GONG BATHS

A Guide to Sound Healing

CONTENTS

ONE

INTRODUCTION

Purpose of this Book

This book tells you what to expect from a gong bath and how best to enjoy and benefit from one. It explains what happens, tells you what to bring along and even how to evaluate what type of gong bath you are attending – a healing one, or simply a relaxing one. In the Appendix and online, there are also advice pages on how you may find one near you.

For those wishing to perform their own gong baths, it tells you how best to prepare for and conduct one, how to play a gong, how to be sensitive to and interact with a gong, how to generate and use its power for your own benefit and the benefit of others, and provides a few cautionary words where necessary.

Background

Sacred sounds have been used and studied since before language. Most religions and spiritual disciplines employ sound or music to enhance their experience of their Creator, and many are aware that the background sound (or vibration, if you prefer) of the Universe is a collective hum.

Pythagoras, who lived for around eighty years until 500 B.C., is the first person in Western scientific and intellectual tradition known to have employed sound for healing purposes, using melodies, harmonies, chants and paeans (or songs). He also spoke of each and every atom producing a particular sound, to collectively form a universal harmony.

Shamans, mystics, priests and ascetics here and elsewhere throughout the world have healed using sticks, drums, gongs, bowls and vocal instruments for thousands of years, largely ignored or marginalized by science.

Sound has been used in many forms to assist meditation, healing or to enhance spiritual experience for thousands of years. The video here gives you some idea of its often-hidden place in the Christian tradition: http://cymatica.com/2013/06/22/rosslyn-chapel-cymatics-video/.

Sound Healing

Instruments used in sound healing include drums, bowls, bells, voices, as well as a gong. Each has its own peculiarities of sound wave, frequency, use and effect.

Sacred sounds bring physical, mental, emotional and spiritual benefits to anyone listening to them or experiencing them. We all know sound and especially musical sound is useful to relax, quiesce, entrance, arouse or energize. We have all probably experienced moments of great joy or deep sadness when listening to music. And many of us have enjoyed a feeling of wholeness or of the deepest gratitude and satisfaction as a result of singing, chanting or playing sacred sounds.

Less well-known is that sound vibrations directly affect liquid bodies, including our own and very obviously our blood, creating complex and beautiful wave patterns. The study of these effects and of any therapeutic benefits, is called cymatics. You can see pictures of these effects at www.cymatics.org, and also at the website noted above (www.cymatica.com), among others.

The author is a member of the American School of Cymatics, which is devoted to its study (http://cymatics.ning.com/profile/StephenJHIll). Their system is not very secure however, judging by the number of phishing emails I receive via their site.

Gong Baths

Gong Baths are a form of sound healing gaining in popularity in Western countries, especially so during the years since the millennium. Gong baths are now held on a regular, even daily basis in most cities and many smaller towns. Attendees' reasons for returning range from relaxation, through physical and emotional cleansing, to spiritual enhancement or enlightenment.

The term "Gong Bath" is potentially misleading: the word "Bath" refers not to the use of water but to the all-embracing effect on us of the sounds produced. A listener bathes in sound in the sense that he or she is surrounded and absorbed by sound vibrations emanating from a gong or gongs, while remaining passive and even asleep.

TWO

WHAT TO EXPECT

Participation

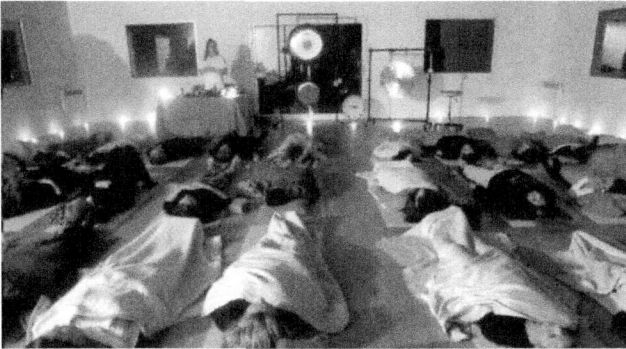

Gong baths are typically held in a hall with enough room for between ten and forty people. Rooms are usually but not necessarily warm with candles or subdued lighting to enhance the experience, as in the above pictures. Advance booking is often requested but rarely demanded. Arrival and settling down in a timely manner are expected, and polite.

Outdoor formats also exist, often as part of larger events, although my personal experience with these is that they have more to do with showmanship than relaxation and healing. Lying down and relaxing in the open air on a warm summer's day is itself relaxing: if that's all you need, there's no need to pay extra.

A Gong Bath takes many forms. The most popular form is a single player and a single gong, usually lasting between thirty minutes and one hour and often held at the end of a yoga class, event or retreat. Some are held over lengthy periods, throughout a whole night for example, or over a whole day or more. Longer gong baths typically use multiple gongs and players, often with participants taking it in turns to be the 'player'.

All are best experienced lying down, relaxing on a yoga or rush mat while covered by a blanket, with eyes closed and head resting on and supported by a pillow or cushion. Additional supports or comforts may be brought, especially by those attendees with physical ailments.

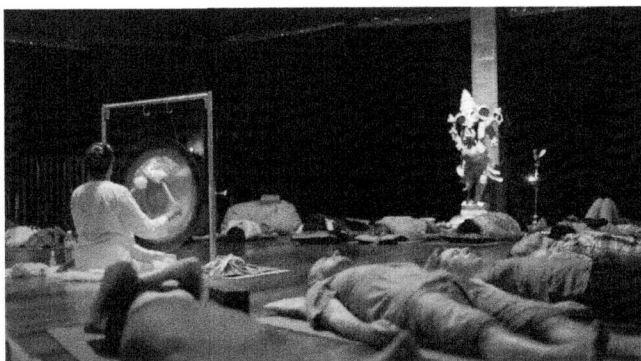

There is no need to lie down, particularly if you find the position uncomfortable or unnerving. A gong bath experienced sitting or standing will still be beneficial, albeit less relaxing. Provided moving around or changing position is done quietly and with respect for others, it is usually but not always permitted – it is best to check in advance.

Audience participants often fall asleep, which makes little difference to their experience – sound vibrations pass through and interact with their physical and spiritual bodies whether awake or asleep.

The organizer or host, which I shall call the Gong Master for ease of reference, will usually provide some words of introduction. These typically include a description of the particular gong (or gongs) and its effects, the likely duration, whether or not it is permissible to move about, etc, as well as the usual hygiene factors like location of toilets, emergency exits and so on. He will also likely ask about the audience's previous experience of gong baths, if he has not already garnered this information at time of booking.

There is usually a brief pause while everyone settles down. As soon as the room falls silent, the Gong Master will begin.

The first minute or two is usually neither intense nor loud, especially if there are a number of 'first-timers'.

Depending upon the overall duration, this period may be extended to last perhaps ten minutes or more. In part this is to allow ears to become accustomed to the nature of the sound, and to allow them time to adjust to the volume. Mostly however, it is to avoid emotionally sensitive souls from being overwhelmed.

The best term to describe such a reaction is 'existential shock'. Its cause is most often that an attendee has been in an over-anxious or troubled state of mind for some time beforehand, and this is the first moment they have actually relaxed for weeks or even months. Such a person is strictly speaking not reacting to the gong but to themselves – they would have had this reaction however they first chose to relax.

It may be that such attendees have not before experienced such a sudden or strong release of deep emotions, or it may be because they are experiencing a profound, new experience. Whatever the reason, the event is intended to be relaxing and releasing, which is best done gradually and under control rather than in an unsettling rush.

If the gong bath is well-run by an experienced Gong Master, the intensity will gradually increase to reach a peak, usually around one third to one half of the way through its overall duration. In graphical terms, where the x-axis is intensity and the y-axis is time, this would mean either a normal curve or a left-skewed curve.

The sensations experienced by an attendee are likely to mirror the relevant curve of intensity, although not necessarily so. If one remains awake, one may feel a varying range of emotions arising, or may experience a profound sense of well-being. If your eyes remain closed then colors, patterns or images may appear. Memories may surface, sometimes painful, sometimes pleasurable. These are all signs that the gong bath is performing its magic: releasing emotions and blockages while in a relaxed state that an attendee may choose to examine or ignore.

Many experienced participants will sleep through the entire event. If asleep, one may well experience intense dreams, perhaps involving some kind of connection with your higher self. The relaxing and releasing effects will still occur during sleep, as later reflection will confirm.

The gong bath ends in silence. There is no clapping or similar expression of appreciation: many are asleep and those who are awake will have fallen silent. The silence usually lasts five to ten minutes, until a few people moving arms and legs or gradually waking up act as a signal for the Gong Master to end the session.

Sometimes the Gong Master will say a few closing words but usually not more than a thank you and a blessing, or similar. Packing-up typically begins and progresses in a slow and quiet manner, with no one wishing to disturb the peaceful aura in the room.

It is advisable not to rush away at the end but to remain at least fifteen minutes before departing, especially by car. Most hall bookings will accommodate this delay. One's mental state will be relaxed and open. It should be enjoyed and indulged for maximum physical, mental and spiritual benefit. The risk of accident while in this relaxed state is increased.

Sometimes CD recordings of gong baths are available for sale. In my experience such recordings have no healing effect whatever, nor do I find them in the least relaxing (although I have heard others tell me they find them so). Generally, I find them irritating.

NOTE: Some gong baths involve multiple gong sessions, often lasting a whole day or night with participants taking it in turns to perform. They are most often held as events for specialists, that is, experienced Gong Masters, although not exclusively so.

Preparation

Anyone can attend. There are no physical or mental preparations that are an absolute pre-requisite. However, abstinence from consuming meat, and especially from alcohol or non-prescription drugs is recommended for at least twenty-four hours before attending. This will enable a more complete relaxed or meditative state to be induced within you.

It is also beneficial to sit or meditate quietly for a few minutes in advance, and to avoid any state of agitation or hurrying-in at the last minute. Again there is no absolute requirement, but your level of enjoyment and healing is much enhanced if you are already somewhat relaxed. Gong baths are often preceded by a yoga session or at least by some simple stretching, precisely for this reason.

Unless you specifically wish to avoid lying down, ensure you bring a yoga mat or equivalent (two is often preferable, depending upon the state and temperature of flooring), as well as a blanket and pillow. An eye shade or cover may also be desirable, although lighting is anyway likely to be subdued.

If you are not intending to lie down, it is still possible to gain benefit from a gong bath. However, you should examine your real motivation for not wishing to do so. Is the true source of your discomfort actually physical? Or is it because of an innate dislike or fear of relaxing? It is possible to be attracted to the idea of relaxing, while actually leading a lifestyle or having a mental attitude that precludes the possibility. If you suspect the latter, you should seek the counsel of the Gong Master in advance or, better still, seek experience or training in meditation or mindfulness.

Meditation in particular will assist you in adjusting your mental attitude. Your higher self is in effect telling you to attend a gong bath to help you relax and realize your true nature, and your bodily self is likely resisting out of habit.

Effects

A gong bath will do you no physical harm. The sound vibrations will enter and pass through your physical and spiritual body, inducing positive change within your physical and inner being.

Sound healing gong baths work on multiple levels: physical, mental and spiritual. Physical effects may include muscle relaxation and associated pain relief. Mental effects may include visions of colors, clear and well-defined images, or swirling patterns, or intense dreams. The profound relaxation may in turn release emotions and feelings that have been held in check for many years, and you may experience these either positively or negatively.

Most people experience a profound sense of goodness and well-being. Less common is for an attendee to become tearful as repressed emotions surface, often for the first time since some earlier trauma or current drama. Whether experienced negatively or positively, this relaxing and releasing experience bestows considerable physical and mental benefits on a listener.

Sound-healing gong baths may also be profound spiritual experiences, showing or reminding us of another layer of our existence, of our true or essential nature. Experiencing visions of patterns or of the colors purple or violet during a gong bath are indicators of your increased sensitivity to this, and you may find at the time or over subsequent days that your belief patterns change to encompass an expanded consciousness.

You will perhaps become aware of the presence of your higher self, or possibly experience it as an awareness of a deeper realm, or of your etheric body. In Chakra terminology, blockages are frequently opened, especially at the higher levels.

Cautionary Words

Not everyone's experience of gong baths is immediately positive, even if it provides precisely the relaxing and releasing effects they need. If an attendee has been in an over-anxious state for some time, they may find the release of emotions and sensations overwhelming, no matter how slowly or carefully a Gong Master controls the intensity. If you believe you fall into this category, it is worth seeking advice beforehand and perhaps meditating on occasion over a few days beforehand.

If an attendee has a mental illness or perhaps a profound aversion or fear, these may manifest as a fear of relaxation or a denial of emotions. Such people will likely find the whole experience unsettling or disturbing. They will consequently continue to deny or reject the feelings and energy arising, because it does not fit into their negative worldview, which will lead to physical and psychological discomfort.

Sometimes attendees going through emotional pain (for example, a separation or divorce) will find themselves crying uncontrollably. This may be part of a necessary healing process but is nonetheless an uncomfortable experience, especially since it is public.

Not all gong baths are run by Gong Masters. There are no professional qualifications, nor is there any recognized body defining or supervising standards, although there are now schools investigating and reporting upon the effects of sound healing – the American School of Cymatics is one. As for all pastimes growing in popularity, it attracts people more interested in appearances and monetary reward than in the benefit to attendees.

If you feel none of the healing effects described in this book, it is likely you are attending one being run by someone who is not wise or experienced enough to know the difference between relaxation and release, nor sensitive or powerful enough to interact with the gong in the manner described herein. It is still possible to enjoy their gong baths as relaxation and perhaps releasing events, but no spiritual healing will be involved.

THREE

GONG SELECTION

General Information

There are a large range of gongs commercially available, produced in many different countries especially including Germany, China and Japan. They are manufactured and tuned by hand, usually to very high standards as dictated by tradition. Their size, appearance, decoration, qualities of tone and timbre as well as the depth and range of vibrations vary considerably.

Wikipedia has several pages listing various types of gong, although very few of these types are typically used in gong baths:

https://en.wikipedia.org/wiki/Gong#Chau_gong_(Tam-tam)

Size affects the volume and depth of sound, with larger gongs being required for playing in halls or outdoors. Small gongs may be more suitable for playing in smaller rooms or studios, although the cheap ones may produce an unpleasant, tinny sound. Some cheaper gongs are produced using inferior materials and methods and are best avoided.

Manufacturers present their wares via a website. Hence, you may simply use one of the popular search engines like Google to obtain a list of all available types of gong. The Paiste website (http://www.paistegongs.com) for example provides a range of information about the gongs they manufacture. Most Gong Baths I have attended in Europe have used one or more of their Symphonic, Planet, or Sound Creation gongs.

Selection

Access to and experience of playing a range of gongs is helpful when targeting particular physical, mental or spiritual ailments. However, in competent hands all good-quality gongs offer relaxation and releasing, and a good Gong Master will act as a channel for appropriate healing energy, no matter which gong he is using.

If you are choosing a gong for the first time, it is advisable to either arrange a visit to a gong sales center or to attend a short training course. Both will provide you with an opportunity to play and interact with various gongs.

Do not buy a gong simply because it is the only one you have played or because someone else has recommended it to you.

It is possible to select a gong through a logical consideration of its stated effects and of your requirements or experience. However, such an approach is unlikely to lead to you becoming a healer, since it is avoiding the true nature of the gongs and their sound. Better to play a few gongs, feel the effect on you and within you, and to interact with its vibrations. This will familiarize you with its capabilities before purchase. If you meditate before purchasing, you should find that the name of a gong will come to you and you will be in no doubt that this is the gong you should buy.

There is a second-hand market in gongs. They are regularly advertised, usually online via Facebook, Gumtree or equivalents. All the usual cautions about on-line purchases apply. In addition, it is strongly recommended that you test the gong yourself before purchase. Sellers will offer to send you a sound file but this is no use whatever in telling you the quality and qualities of the gong, since none of the effects transmit via this medium.

There are fakes, cheaply manufactured, that produce a very thin range of sound. Also, second-hand gongs may have been used for other than healing purposes and may thus retain negative energy that will change its effectiveness. It is worth asking about how and when a gong has been used, and use your intuition about whether what you are being told is truthful. A gong may be 'cleansed' by your own playing, but it does take a few days for such history to be removed.

For those experienced in meditation, the best way to choose a gong is to meditate deeply and then see what name arises. It may announce itself immediately or it may not do so until you are on the point of ordering, but the name will do so, if you are ready to receive it. A friend of mine was on the telephone ordering a specific gong and, when asked which one she wished to purchase, she spoke a different name. Naturally, she bought that one instead. In summary: don't call them, let your gong call you.

For those not experienced in meditation, some advice and guidance on how to get started with meditating appears later in this book. If you wish to use a gong simply for enjoyment and relaxation, there is no need to practice meditation. If you wish to use a gong for sound healing, the ability to meditate or to feel an awareness of your higher self or of higher realms or levels of existence is a pre-requisite for channeling healing energy. This terminology is explained in the Appendices.

Once you have purchased a gong, it is best to practice with it at home for a few weeks or months before giving any public performance. This will allow an easy familiarity with your gong and its abilities to grow, so that when you are in public you will be better able to intuit or channel any healing.

If you are choosing a second or subsequent gong, you should choose it in the same manner as the first.

FOUR

OTHER EQUIPMENT

There is a range of additional items you will need in order to equip yourself to play a gong, whether in public or on your own. These include a means of striking or stroking the gong, a stand to support it in position while being played, and a means of keeping them all clean.

You will also need a means of letting you know the time or duration of playing, ideally a silent watch or clock, something to sit or rest upon, and a soft blanket or similar on which to rest your mallets to ensure there is minimal noise distraction when placing them down.

Mallets

Mallets is the general term used to describe the various items used to strike or stoke a gong. There is a bewildering array of different types of mallet on the market. They primarily vary by size, weight, and material used for their surface. Their surface may be hard, soft or in-between. They may be flat or round headed. Their heads vary in size from a few millimeters across to several centimeters, and in weight from a few ounces to several pounds. They may come with plain or gnarled handles, with or without thongs, and so on.

In the same way as it is advisable to test several types of gong before you buy, it is wise to test a range of mallets before you choose your first set. Your initial choices will not be a waste of money, one aspect of learning to play the gong is to become familiar with the different sounds and effects made by various weights, surfaces and textures of mallet. Your choices will anyway modify over time.

Examples appear in the following pictures.

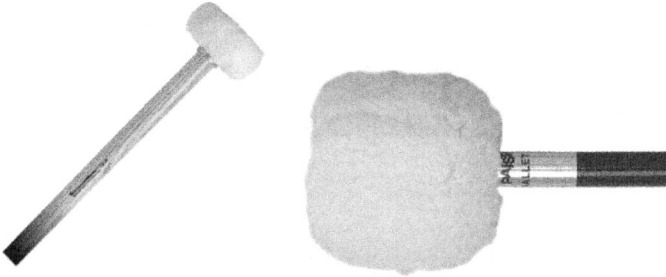

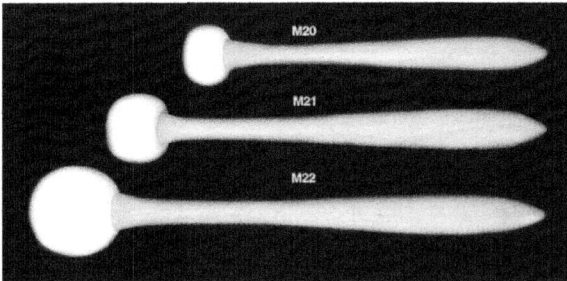

Mallet heads also come in a variety of styles.

Sometimes there is no discernible head, or it may be made of rubber.

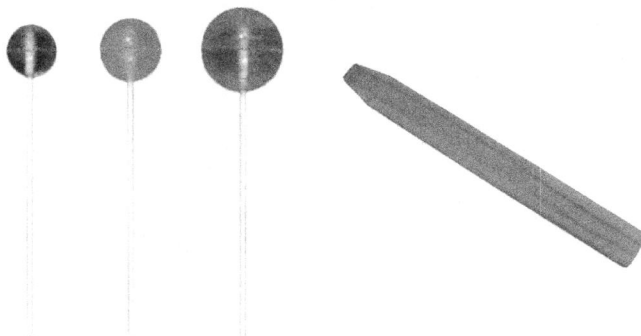

As a general rule, hard surfaces bring forth a harsh, metallic sound while softer surfaces make more mellow, rounded sounds. However, both are capable of making a variety of sounds. Again in general terms, larger, heavier mallets make a deeper and more profound sound than smaller ones. However, both are capable of considerable, overlapping variety.

Bear in mind that many of these mallets and mallet-heads have been developed for orchestral use. This means they may be wholly unsuited for the delicate playing required at times during a gong bath.

In my experience, the cost of a mallet is only indirectly related to the quality of sound it generates, and only slightly related to its durability. In other words, paying a lot for a mallet does not guarantee either its quality of sound or of its construction. There really is no substitute for learning from experience, by practicing with a range and familiarizing yourself with their effects and their ability to handle wear and tear.

Stands

Gongs are heavy, so stands are necessary to support the gong while playing. They must allow free movement of the gong and not interfere or restrict its sound.

There are two principal types of metal or wooden stand: either for standing or for floor-mounting. There are also stands for wall or ceiling mounting. The stands are usually square or rounded in outline, although they may also be intricately carved or decorated. In all cases, a strong cord is required in order to attach and support a gong.

Each gong is manufactured with at least two holes, equidistant either side of its top. A cord is normally strung securely between, which then allows the gong to be mounted for playing. Cords made from various materials are offered by suppliers. I have always found a good quality climbing or marine rope to be the best. They do not interfere with the sound, and they are immensely strong and durable.

Examples follow:

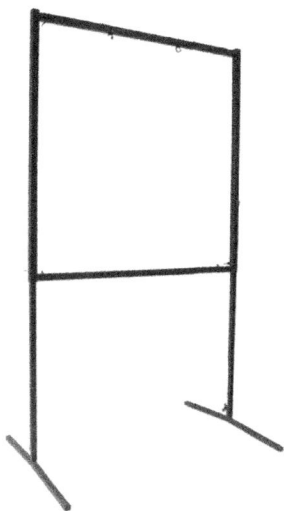

Other Equipment

You should prepare the following for every gong bath you perform.

- A watch or clock to tell the time, which should be silent.
- A seat, blanket or yoga block(s) on which to sit or rest while playing
- A soft, opened blanket or similar on which to rest your mallets, to ensure there is minimal noise distraction when picking them up or placing them down.

Cleaning

When cleaning your gong, it is best to follow your gong manufacturer's instructions, if provided. If none are provided, cleaning should be performed as simply as possible. Use a damp cloth to wipe clean, then dry immediately. Do not use detergents or other surfactants, as this will damage both the finish and the tuning of the gong.

Candle wax or similar non-adhesives may be gently eased away with a fingernail. Grimy or oily streaks or sticky residues from sellotape or adhesives may be removed using gentle strokes with a cotton-bud doused in nail-varnish remover. Using varnish remover entails some risk that the surface shine may diminish but it should not otherwise affect the gong.

Repairs

If your gong is damaged or dented in any way, the best option is to speak to the manufacturer. Some will repair and retune. Self-repairs are fraught with difficulty and should be avoided, unless you have considerable prior experience.

FIVE

LEARNING TO PLAY

Training Courses

Short courses are available that cover the basics of gong playing. These are primarily intended to familiarize you with a gong (or several gongs) and to allow you to spend some time playing one or more gongs. They usually include some "do's and don'ts" of gong baths. They are typically held over one or two days of four to six hours duration, and are useful as a basic introduction.

Some gong masters and sound healers offer additional courses. Some courses offer only a little greater familiarity and experience playing certain gongs and mallets; others are offered as part of a more comprehensive training in sound healing and even as part of a more general healing course. There are courses lasting from a weekend in duration to over 18 months part-time that cover some or all of the principles of sound healing, in its many forms and in varying depths. If you search online for 'sound healing' or similar, a range of courses and events is shown.

I run special courses for gong players interested in gaining the capabilities covered in this book, which may be requested through my website (details at the end of this book). A pre-requisite for attending is prior experience of meditation or, better still, some prior meditation instruction from me.

Practice

Your best option for learning to play a gong is to practice on your own. You should vary the manner and frequency of striking, stroking and touching the gong, experiment with using rhythm or a-rhythmic sound, and familiarize yourself with changes of volume.

While practicing, you may notice how the intensity of effect of the sounds produced by the gong varies, especially if you have meditated before commencing. If you are tired or if your mind wanders while you are playing, you may equally notice how the sound is flat or lacking in intensity. Becoming aware of these changes is the first step to mastering your gong.

The Three Stages of Learning

Stage One

The first step comes when you practice enough and with enough attention to notice the changes in intensity of the effect produced by the sounds coming from the gong.

You may feel this in the form of a sense of excitement, perhaps accompanied by a raised heartbeat or rate of breathing. Equally you may experience this as a state of profound relaxation, or you may become aware of colors, patterns or images affecting you over the day or two following this practice.

However experienced, at this early stage you should use your growing awareness to deliberately produce sounds of different intensity and effect, noticing how the intensity varies with the degree of concentration or preparation (in the form of meditation) you have made.

Experiment first with different means and rates of striking the gong, as well as what happens if you play different parts of the gong at different times. I call this latter exercise 'searching', which is the best word I can find to describe the process of striking the gong in different places to find which part of the gong *at that moment in time* produces the most intense effect.

You should also experiment by playing each hand in turn, as each hand will produce a different intensity and different effects from the same part of the gong.

Later, and especially, practice with different personal intentions or levels of attention or concentration, and notice the consequential changes in the quality of sound produced and its effect upon you.

I found this first step to be a very pleasurable experience. In my case, I practiced alone for six months before I even considered performing in public. By the end of this time I had learned how to control the intensity and effect of the gong, and could use the gong to interact with my own feelings and emotions, healing myself.

Stage Two

This is the second stage of learning: using the energy generated by the gong to interact with your own feelings, emotions and beliefs.

I had already been meditating for some years prior to taking up the gong and I knew something of what to expect. However, it still came as a surprise how easily and strongly the interaction happened.

Certain sounds or sequences of sounds produced either a deep sense of relaxation, or a heightened sense of excitement and expectation. Later, I realized that my mood was profoundly different by the end of each session: generally more balanced and forgiving of others. My heart rate had also slowed.

It is important to note that the energy being directed (or channeled, if you prefer) is universal energy. This energy does not originate from within us, except insofar as we are a tiny part of the universal. Because it is universal, this energy is accessible to all.

Once you understand the meaning of those statements, which is explained in more detail in the Appendices, and once you are comfortable that you can control how your gong-playing interacts with your own emotions and feelings, then you are ready as a healer to play the gong in public for the first time.

Stage Three

The third stage of learning involves and requires an awareness of how the effects of your gong-playing interact between the gong, yourself and your audience, collectively and individually. The link between these is the universal energy being directed or channeled by you through the gong. The sound healing energy will radiate, transmit and be received through you, but its origin is everywhere.

If you are already sensitive to Reiki or other healing energies then you should readily feel the energy, although your understanding of what you are experiencing may be colored by any prior understanding or belief that the energy involved somehow emanates from you. Any such belief is mistaken and should be discarded.

Because of my experience of meditation in company and therefore my awareness of group consciousness, I knew in advance something of what to expect from this third stage of learning. Even so, when I performed in public for the first time, the immediacy and strength of my interaction (through the gong) with the audience came as a great surprise to me.

My playing of the gong was directing energy through me to the gong and thence to the audience, and that interaction was both affecting the audience and affected by the audience, via a kind of feedback. That it all happened so readily and immediately was the great surprise!

Once you have mastered this third stage of learning and can control the intensity, duration and manner of the energy being channeled, then you have become a Gong Master capable of healing others in a safe, controlled manner.

You do not have to worry about whether the energy is doing 'good' – such universal energy is always appropriate to each individual member of your audience.

The audience may not all or immediately experience it positively, some may even have negative visions or experiences or feel the urge to 'flee' this new experience, but be assured that even in this case the energy channeled by the gong is releasing something within each individual that needs to be released. That they as individuals may not be ready to receive the healing only serves to show just how much they need it.

Additional Awareness

At some point during the three stages noted above, you may notice that the intensity of the healing effect varies according to the lunar calendar, or to some other life cycle. You may also notice that the intensity and nature of sounds produced are affected by the relative number and strength of male and female energies in your audience, which energies are not necessarily or directly related to their physical sex.

I quickly became aware of the male and female influence, primarily because my left (feminine) hand often predominated when men are present in number, whereas the opposite occurred otherwise. Left-handed playing provides a fulfilling and balancing energy for the masculine energy, and vice versa for the right-hand.

I only became aware of the influence of the lunar cycle after I was well into the third stage of learning and regularly performing gong baths in public on at least a weekly basis. It became obvious that the energy was very different during a full moon, stronger and at the same time more feminine in nature.

Learning to Play Summary

Stage One – familiarize yourself with various means of playing the gong and experience how the intensity varies.

Stage Two – familiarize yourself with how the intensity affects your own feelings, emotions, sensitivities and beliefs, both while playing and later. Especially notice any changes in your attitude or demeanor.

Stage Three – familiarize yourself with how the energy being channeled by you is affected by and affects members of an audience, in all four of the categories of feelings, emotions, sensitivities and beliefs. Meditate regularly and trust the universe to produce only healing energy.

Lastly keep your mind open to other effects, such as the lunar cycle.

SIX

GONG TECHNIQUES

Posture

It is possible to play a gong while standing, sitting or kneeling. The likelihood of a gong bath being relaxing is the same for all three basic positions.

Contrary to popular belief, it is possible to be in a meditative state while fully conscious and aware of your surroundings. However, it is difficult to do so and requires training and practice, especially if standing and with your eyes open.

If a Gong Player is standing, the likelihood is therefore reduced of a gong bath being more than relaxing. That is, it may not be effective at releasing of emotions, blockages, etc.. This is because the chances of their interacting meaningfully with the gong is reduced, since they are less likely to be in or close to a meditative state while performing.

If a Gong Player is standing, the likelihood of a gong bath inducing any kind of spiritual state or experience is similarly reduced, again because it is much less likely they are in or close to a deep meditative state.

A seated position for playing is generally preferable, with your back erect, neck relaxed and arms free to move. You may sit cross-legged or with feet to each side, or in any other position you find comfortable. As a general rule, whatever position you find most suitable for meditation is likely the best posture for you to adopt while playing a gong.

My preferred position is seated, normally with my legs to each side rather than crossed. This is very much a personal preference: most of my meditation is performed while in Virasana (Hero pose), rather than with legs crossed or linked as in Sukhasana (Easy pose), Siddhasana (Accomplished pose) or Padmasana (Lotus pose).

I often stand for the first minute or so of playing, especially if there are some audience members who have never before attended a gong bath. The reason for this is that standing ensures that the effect of playing is less intense. This ensures the attendees enjoy a gentle introduction to the sound of the gong, without being immediately overwhelmed by its unanticipated intense effects.

For the same reason I often end a gong bath by standing for the last few minutes, which in effect guarantees a gradual return from a possibly intense experience.

Breathing

Deep, steady breathing is important during playing. This is partly because playing for an hour or more may involve considerable physical exertion, but mostly because it guarantees the mental state of a gong player.

Correct breathing is also important during preparation for a gong bath, as it will aid the inducement of a meditative state in a gong player, thus allowing him to better perform any interaction with a gong.

I find a minute or two of Ujjayi breathing to be ideal as a preparation: most books on yoga and many online journals will provide detailed guidance on how to perform this correctly. A brief summary is in the Appendix.

Grip

The best way to hold a mallet is gently between forefinger and thumb, with the remaining fingers providing support as necessary. This allows both subtle and strong movements of the wrist, and arm if required. It also allows you to strike, stroke, or remain touching the gong with a mallet. I normally use both hands.

Holding a mallet too tightly will result in fatigue in your arms, wrist and hand, and possibly in cramp or pain, especially if playing for an extended period. It is also important to ensure your shoulders remain relaxed: consciously lower them at intervals if you feel any tightness creeping in.

If a mallet has a cord attached, ensure it does not swing loosely as this may strike the gong and make a discordant, interruptive sound.

Strike

Striking a gong means impacting the surface of a gong with a mallet in a single, often rapid movement. Contact is momentary. Subsequent removal of the mallet from the point of impact occurs almost instantaneously.

A single strike contact is often sharp, with the resulting sound being left to resonate for a few seconds afterwards.

Multiple strike contacts typically form part of a series, where the resulting sounds from each individual strike mingle and coalesce with the others. These may form rhythmical patterns, or not.

Stroke

Stroking a gong means dragging the surface of a mallet across part of the surface of a gong, usually for a relatively short duration, inducing a variety of sounds.

The manner of stroking a gong is much the same whatever type of mallet is being used. Stroking with a soft-headed mallet will likely induce a quiet but continuous and often high-pitched sound, while stroking with a hard or solid mallet surface will likely produce a loud, screeching sound.

Touch

Touching a gong with a mallet means holding the surface of the mallet against the surface of the gong for a period of time. The duration of this period may vary considerably from a few milliseconds to several seconds.

With a soft-headed mallet the effect is to dampen the volume of sound produced, especially of higher frequencies. It may also shorten the duration of certain sounds.

A hard-headed mallet held lightly against a gong's surface may be used to add a slight reverberation effect.

Volume

The volume of sound emanating from a gong varies considerably during each performance. Care should be taken to ensure that the volume of any sound produced is appropriate to the size of hall or venue in which it is performed, and to the sensitivity and well-being of the audience therein.

If the venue is large and the volume too low, the effect may be reduced and attendees may easily be disturbed by movement, rustling or snoring. If the venue is small and the gong is played too loudly, the sounds will appear harsh and disturbing to the audience, rather than relaxing and releasing.

In my experience, this is the most common mistake made by Gong Players: they equate volume directly with power or intensity, whereas those effects are at most only indirectly related to the volume of playing.

It is always advisable to perform a simple sound test before any gong bath: strike the gong at various volumes and walk around the hall assessing the appropriateness of volume and effect of each strike.

Volume is most directly controlled by the force or speed of impact from a mallet. Hard-headed mallets tend to induce loud, harsh sounds. Soft-headed mallets tend to produce quieter sounds. In both cases, a greater force and speed of striking a gong will induce a higher volume.

Volume may also be increased by the frequency with which a gong is struck. In other words, repeated or continuous striking of a gong increases the breadth and volume of the resulting sound, with each strike adding multiplicatively to the effect.

Lastly, volume may be reduced by touching the gong, as described above.

Rhythm

There is no need for rhythm to be deliberately introduced into any gong bath. However, if one's playing has become entirely intuitive then at some time and perhaps frequently you will find yourself playing rhythmically.

Rhythms may be simple and repetitive and played with a single hand (for example one steady repeated beat 1- 2 - 3 - 4) or complex and varied and played with both hands (for example with one hand playing 3 beats for every 2 beats played by the other hand, in a 3:2 time-signature).

It is best to follow your intuition when you find yourself playing rhythmically, rather than be concerned with any form of rational analysis of its appropriateness. If you are intuitively interacting with your gong, then whatever sounds you are creating are the most appropriate ones for your audience at that time.

Rhythm and repetition have been used for thousands of years as a means of inducing meditative or hypnotic states. I have found myself playing complex rhythms and repetitive rhythms I later recognized as identical to those played in native American rituals. In none of these cases was I deliberately playing rhythmically: they just happened.

Interacting with a gong

Our senses tell us of a world of matter, causality, and other physical laws to obey. However, all of us are in reality energetic and eternal (almost) beings, composed of the same universal energy of which all matter and beings are made. For this reason, we are directly connected to the entire world around us. Therefore, there already exists a connection between you and your gong, between your audience and your gong, and between your audience and you.

Accessing these connections is straightforward but requires using your intuition or feelings, rather than any logic or reasoning. Hence the value of meditation: it teaches us first to relax and thence to access different levels of existence, including the level(s) required for accessing that connection.

If you already understand the two paragraphs above, then you will find interacting with a gong very easy. You will quickly become aware of its effects upon different parts of your physical and spiritual bodies.

If you are not yet aware of the latter of these effects, interacting with your gong will over time enable you to become aware of it, and teach you to communicate and identify with your higher self, which is a pre-requisite for spiritual enhancement.

Whether the direct or indirect route is taken, you will then act as a channel for receiving and passing on healing energy to those in your audience.

If you do not comprehend or accept the first paragraphs in this section, then it will take you a little longer to fully interact with your gong. Perseverance by you will win the day however, since regular practice at playing your gong will allow it to work its magic upon you. It will gradually induce a greater inclination to meditate, ultimately resulting in an awareness of its full effects.

You may initially feel this change in the form of a tingling or other sensation at the various energy centers (or chakras) in your body. Or you may experience vivid dreams or become aware of a heightened intuition.

Our reactions and manner of change and growth are all different but ultimately lead towards the same goal of heightened awareness. All this is normal, and a precursor to becoming aware of the connections through the gong: firstly between you and the universal energy, and secondly (through you and the gong) between your audience and the universal energy.

You are also likely to experience a change in your perception and understanding of the world and its various levels of existence, as your mind adjusts to the new inputs it is receiving.

SEVEN
RUNNING YOUR OWN

Preparation

Personal physical preparation for a gong bath should include a modified diet with no or at least a reduced quantity of meat and alcohol for a whole day beforehand. This will enhance or enable a better connection with a gong.

You should ensure that you have all the necessary items with which to perform. In addition to a gong or gongs, these include a suitable mallet(s), a blanket or similar on which to place the mallets (thus avoiding a disturbing or distracting noise when picking up or replacing mallets), a timepiece such as a small clock or watch, and a low stool or blocks upon which to sit or rest while playing.

You should be careful to remove any loose items of jewelry as these may easily fall or strike a gong, making a disturbing or distracting noise.

Lastly, you should thoroughly check that the location is suitable and in a fit state for people to lie down. Quite often, rented halls are not as clean as one would like, which becomes apparent when a member of the audience places a yoga mat or blanket on the floor.

In addition to ensuring the floor is swept, I find it worthwhile sending Reiki to all four corners of the room, thus removing any negative energy that may have built up from previous occupants and setting in place a positive or sacred space within which your audience may sit or lie.

Mental preparation should include a means of ensuring you are relaxed and with a clear mind are ready to perform. Ideal preparation is a brief period of meditation but even just a few quiet moments alone may suffice.

There is no need to plan any specific form of playing or interacting with the gong: it is far better to let the gong lead you where it needs to go.

Spiritual preparation depends upon your own preferences. Some spend a short time breathing deeply or using some form of pranayama, others may issue a brief prayer or chant.

My own preparation is very simple: I enter a brief but deep meditation and connect to the highest level of our existence, from where I expect and command guidance and a successful outcome for everyone present.

Audience

Some or all members of your audience may have never before attended a gong bath. Even those with prior experience may not have attended one of yours, which may provide a substantially different experience to those they have attended.

Therefore it is always worth beginning a gong bath by saying a few words about who you are, which gong or gongs you are using and what effects the audience may expect to experience. In particular, you should explain if your main aim is relaxation, releasing or some form of sound healing.

The audience will feel more relaxed if you explain the format and duration of the gong bath, and it is worth telling attendees what to do if they feel uncomfortable and need to move around or leave, or if they need to visit the toilet during the gong bath.

I always ask who has and who has not been to a gong bath before. There is usually more than one. This is important to know, as old hands may be at ease with you heading directly into an intense healing session. However, beginners will definitely not be.

Especially where some or all of the audience are unknown to you, it is advisable to adhere to one of the formats outlined earlier. That is, provide both a lengthy warm-up and a lengthy close-down period at the end.

I have found it helpful to ask if anyone has any questions or concerns? On more than one occasion I have been asked whether or not the audience will get wet, which says a lot about the general level of knowledge of what a gong bath involves.

Lastly, it is advisable to remind everyone to turn off their mobile phones.

Beginning

I begin any gong bath by advising people to lie either head towards the gong or feet towards the gong. In my experience, this induces the maximum effect. It is also worthwhile telling everyone they can be as close to or as far from the gong as they wish, within the constraints of the room or hall.

Once everyone has settled onto their mat or blanket (or chair), the points made in the 'Audience' section above about getting to know your audience and helping them to feel comfortable should be covered.

Once you are happy that all questions and concerns have been dealt with, you should instruct everyone to lie down (or sit) and settle under blankets etc., making themselves as comfortable as possible.

Once the noise of any rustling or shifting position or rearranging pillows has subsided, you may begin to play.

The first minute or so of playing should always be used to get attendees used to the sound of the gong. During this period play quietly and slowly, gradually increasing volume (and pace of beating, if relevant) to somewhere around half of your intended or expected maximum.

If there are novice attendees, you should extend this initial period up to five minutes or longer, and especially avoid introducing any profound, healing moments.

Duration

It is worth deciding upon the approximate duration of the gong bath well in advance, even publishing this in any flyers. You may vary the duration according to what you experience during the gong bath and extend it if necessary to achieve the desired effect.

If added on to some other event such as a yoga class, a gong bath is typically of thirty minutes or so duration. This length may extend to between one and two hours or longer, if billed as a special event on its own.

Expecting people to lie still for up to two hours is wishful and likely to induce cramp or other pains. It is therefore more beneficial to offer a program that includes a few stretching and bending exercises before the gong bath begins, since this will prepare attendees' bodies for lying down and enable their minds to relax prior to commencement.

The law of diminishing returns also applies, and there is little utility in prolonging any one gong session beyond about forty-five minutes duration. I usually deliver gong baths of between thirty-minutes and fifty-minutes duration, with some stretching, meditation or other preparation beforehand.

Intensity

Once the initial period has ended, it is best to gradually increase intensity rather than to provide and sudden change. Sudden changes are surprising and may even be shocking for the audience, and may cause a negative reaction. This is often felt by an attendee as an increase in heart rate and release of adrenalin. Sudden changes in volume or speed of beating should also be avoided, for similar reasons

It is advisable to reach the climax of your healing intensity somewhere between forty per cent and sixty-five percent of the way through the entire duration of the gong bath. The duration of this climax may vary considerably but plenty of time should be allowed for adjustment before and after the highest intensity period.

Your intuition should inform you as to the optimum intensity and duration of healing and playing for any audience. You must learn to trust it, rather than stick to some pre-determined plan. Even so, there are constraints determined by audience expectations: they may already have made plans that require a timely departure from the event.

Ending

A gradual reduction in intensity should be followed by a similarly gradual reduction in volume and probably of speed or tempo, especially if you have played rhythmically during the gong bath. This will allow time for any healing to have begun and for any adjustment back to normal for those most affected. It should also allow an attendee to finish in a relaxed state, no matter how intense any healing has been during the gong bath.

When finishing, it is advisable not to cause any noise through your own movement or replacing of mallets, and certainly not by beginning to pack away any items. Loud or incongruous noises will easily spoil the relaxed mood of your participants, especially if they are woken from a deep sleep.

EIGHT
PRACTICE

Initial

Your practice regime should include an initial concentration on becoming familiar with your gong, especially on the different sounds and effects that you can induce through different styles and texture of playing. Thereafter, practice should be in accordance with the guidelines written earlier in the "Learning to play a Gong" section.

Ongoing

Once fully familiar with your gong(s), it is worthwhile continuing to practice. Continued, regular practice will ensure you remain in touch with the capabilities of your gong and with your own healing abilities, as expressed through playing the gong. A personal practice should be seen as a pleasure and even a joy, rather than any form of chore.

Your relationship with your gong will vary over time and, with regular practice, increase in depth and intensity. Become fully aware of how you interact with your gong when alone. When you then play in public, you will become increasingly aware of the interaction between you, your gong and your audience. You will literally feel the energy flowing between all three.

Over time, you will even be able to identify the interaction between individual members of your audience and you, via your gong. Always remember though that the source of this energy is Universal, not from within you.

NINE

EVALUATION

Your Own

It is worth taking the time after a gong bath to run through what happened during the entire event, to evaluate whether it met your objectives and intentions, whether and how the audience benefitted, and so on.

Questions to ponder include:

- Could I have said anything different in my introduction that would have made the event even more enjoyable for participants?
- Did I understand and adequately consider the interests and abilities of the attendees?
- Was the beginning section of my playing lengthy enough for the less-experienced attendees?

- Judging from their reaction, was the intensity of my playing suited to the audience?
- How much negative energy within certain members of the audience did I sense?
- Did I allow sufficient time at the end for people to enjoy the relaxation period?

In addition, I like to consider the type of gong playing that resulted from our (my gong and me) interaction with the audience. Especially with regard to whether or not my left or right-hand was dominant, whether or not it was primarily or exclusively rhythmical or a-rhythmical, and whether or not I sensed other forces at play.

I have used this mental exercise to amend and improve the gong baths I have conducted. A change in my standard format resulted, one which now varies depending upon audience and venue.

Others

It is best to avoid any negative thoughts about another person's gong-playing abilities. Any gong bath played with good intent will have a relaxing and probably a releasing effect. If the gong player is not as capable of healing as you then it is better to forgive them and wish them well in their journey, rather than feel disappointed or let-down.

That said, there are some clear pointers that are worth noting when evaluating any gong bath, including your own:

Q

Did it achieve its stated objective for you – whether relaxation, releasing, or healing?

Q

Was the whole event run professionally, without inappropriate interruption?

Q

Were instructions and guidance as clear as possible, and did everyone know what to expect?

Q

Was there consideration given for those unused to such events?

Q

Was the cost worth the experience?

TEN

COMMERCIAL

Advertising

Advertising your gong bath may be conducted in a variety of ways. If you already perform other forms of healing or teach yoga or similar, then your present customers and classes will certainly be interested, to the extent that you may need not advertise further. Word-of-mouth works well.

Facebook and other social media sites are a good means of publicizing an event, whether regular or occasional. In addition I have found local magazines to be helpful, especially when accompanied by an explanatory editorial piece or a picture.

The hall or studio you are likely using for the event will normally have a notice board or similar, upon which you should place a large flyer. A good friend of mine printed several hundred postcard size leaflets and personally delivered them door-to-door within a two-mile radius of her regular event.

Bookings

Booking is easiest done online, using any of a multitude of booking services such as Bookwhen, Simplybook.me, Bookeo, etc etc. The best way to find one to suit yourself is to search online for a class booking system, and trial those that seem to offer the best terms and functionality.

They all have the facility to take payments online for individual, group or repeat bookings, and most include discounting and refund options within their standard price. Payment is usually by credit card or Paypal or similar. I cannot recommend any particular one, since each varies slightly and may be suited to your particular needs. Always be careful to set the maximum number of attendees who may book any venue or event, to avoid disappointment and make any payments-on-the-door more expensive and subject to availability.

If for a single event, you may wish to preclude refunds within 24 hours of the event. If you are arranging a regular event, you may find it helpful to offer a single trial date and thereafter customers can only book a series of specific dates. Having already paid to attend usually acts as a sufficient incentive to avoid suffering last-minute dropouts because some other issue or event or poor weather has occurred.

CD Sales

I have listened to a number of CD recordings of gong baths, as well as various YouTube video and audio offerings. None of them have had the slightest effect on me, nor should we expect them to do so. By definition they are past events, unrelated to our present situation or condition and with no interaction possible between gong, player and audience. Any claimed effect is therefore illusory. They are thus a complete waste of time and money, which is why I never offer any for sale.

ELEVEN
OTHER PATHS

There are other means of sound healing, including crystal bowls, Tibetan bowls, human voice, and tuning forks.

Crystal Bowls

Crystal bowls come in a variety of sizes and require some knowledge of technique to play successfully, generating a single non-complex note. I have found them to be profoundly relaxing, easily inducing a deep state of meditation or sleep.

Tibetan Bowls

Also known by other names such as singing bowls. As for crystal bowls except they are generally made from various combinations of metals and alloys, usually decorated.

Chanting

The human voice has a deeply relaxing and spiritually profound effect upon most of us. This is especially true if you participate actively in the chanting. The actual sound, phrase or words used will vary the effect upon a participant, even if any phrase or sound is in a language unknown to you.

In my experience the deepest meditative and spiritual effects always occur using the single sound 'OM'. Others report widely differing experiences, from a wide variety of sounds and methods.

Tuning Forks

These are pretty much what they say on the tin. Once struck, they produce a single note that sounds for a considerable duration before being struck again. I confess to finding these irritating rather than relaxing or releasing

APPENDICES

GONG EXAMPLES

I have included below some examples of good-quality Planet gongs, together with a brief description of their characteristics and various effects as stated by their manufacturers or others, and as experienced by the author.

My experience of playing a particular gong often concurs with the stated description of its effects, but does not always do so. Any such descriptions should be taken as a guide only and you should always verify any claim about their effects using your own experience and intuition.

CHIRON GONG

Characteristics

Colour: Blue/Turquoise 151.27Hz

Chakra: Throat and third eye

Pitch: D#

Astrological: Virgo

Character: Initiation

General Effects

Chiron is a healer of deep wounds. Unconventional and non-traditional, it accesses our deepest wounds. It also helps initiate us into becoming Healers. It can help us to find meaning in turmoil and pain, whether within a relationship or through one of our talents.

Author's Comments

My experience of playing this gong confirms it as powerful and very capable of healing, helping a listener to recognize what requires healing within them, and to identify what a healing process requires of them. It is especially powerful for releasing abilities or feelings related to communication, clairvoyance or intuition.

EARTH GONG

Characteristics

Colour: Blue/Green 136.10Hz

Chakra: Throat

Pitch: C#

Astrological: Earth's Yearly Seasonal Cycle

Character: nature, nurture, Mother

General Effects

The Earth Gong brings us into harmony with the movement of the Earth, providing balance and space needed to complete our destiny. The pitch of C# is the original sound of Om and the pitch of all sacred Eastern instruments, connecting us with any who work with sacred sound. It fosters creativity, spiritual relaxation, balance, alignment and renewal.

Author's Comments

I would sum up this gong's effect in a single word: balance. It helps us to be sure we are on the right path and in the right place, balancing both our need to be grounded in day-to-day reality as well as nurturing awareness of our true, spiritual nature. It helps to ensure we are in harmony with our physical and spiritual surroundings.

EARTH SIDEREAL DAY GONG

Characteristics

Colour: Red 194.71Hz

Chakra: Root

Pitch: G

Astrological: All signs, single day

Character: Vitality, freedom, energy, the self

General Effects

This gong is stimulating and energizing, helping us pursue our destiny. It represents the passing of a single day on Earth and is especially good for focus and for morning meditation. It will dislodge suppressed emotions or energy blocks, especially in the lower chakras, making one feel alive.

Author's Comments

Excellent for releasing suppressed emotions and beliefs.

JUPITER GONG

Characteristics

Colour: Violet 183.6Hz

Chakra: Crown

Pitch: F#

Astrological: Sagittarius/Pisces

Character: Evolution

General Effects

Jupiter will open you up, check and affirm the correct journey for your soul. It is a patriarchal force and a tough fearless spiritual teacher, but with faith and grace its tone will expand your spirit with a gentle easy mastery.

Author's Comments

This gong is excellent as a channel for releasing, especially of emotions or for blockages in the higher chakras. Use in conjunction with regular, deep meditation.

MARS GONG

Characteristics

Colour: Blue 144.7Hz

Chakra: Brow or third eye

Pitch: D

Astrological: Aries/Scorpio

Character: Passion

General Effects

Mars will help you achieve your earthly spiritual and physical goals by better marshalling and directing your energy. It offers courage, self-mastery and aids decisiveness, adding excitement and energising.

Author's Comments

This gong exudes masculine energy. This will increase the energy level and desire for personal growth of any listener.

SATURN GONG

Characteristics

Colour: Blue 147.9Hz

Chakra: Brow

Pitch: D

Astrological: Capricorn/Aquarius

Character: Stability, patience, structure, self-discipline, protection.

General Effects

Saturn helps us to establish healthy boundaries and forges discipline within us, so we may gain the power and wisdom to actualize our soul's purpose. Saturn creates perseverance and promotes integrity.

Author's Comments

My experience with this gong is somewhat different to the above, being primarily about acceptance and patience. It is profoundly cleansing and releasing at all levels, helping listeners to comprehend limitations they have imposed upon themselves as well as to identify or refine their true purpose.

In addition to promoting acceptance and patience, it helps to balance and align masculine and feminine tendencies within each of us.

SUN GONG

Characteristics

Colour: Yellow 126.22Hz

Chakra: Solar plexus/Heart

Pitch: B

Astrological: Leo

Character: Self

General Effects

The Sun Gong is the heart of our Universe. It brings great energy and healing with its radiance and power. It purifies with its light and cuts through negativity. From its tones all things are possible. Its sounds will take safely beyond your minds limited comprehension to a place unimagined.

Author's Comments

This gong is excellent for removing negative attitudes or beliefs, especially those affecting or affected by our heart or restricting our ability to manifest and enjoy our lives on earth.

NIBIRU GONG

Characteristics

Colour: 161.26 Yellow

Chakra: whole body/Aura

Pitch: E

Astrological: Libra

Character: evolution enlightenment

General Effects

Nibiru promotes awareness of our true nature, and helps us identify our emotional needs, weaknesses and longing. To achieve resolution and enlightenment we can then repair and restore ourselves to balance. A healer and transformer.

Author's Comments

My first experience with this gong was startling. It is powerful, and especially helpful in bringing soul and past life issues to the surface.

OTHER GONGS

Other gongs in common use include Mercury, Neptune, Platonic Year Earth Gong, Pluto, Sedna, Sidereal Moon, Symphonic, Synodic Moon, Uranus and Venus.

You may also find various other gongs represented. A comprehensive list of gong types appears in Wikipedia, as noted earlier in this section.

QUICK GUIDES

BREATHING

Practicing deep, steady breathing provides many benefits, well documented in yoga books and manuals. It is also a pre-requisite for anyone wishing to play a gong for healing purposes.

You may learn all about yogic breathing methods by reading or searching online for "Pranayama". However, I strongly recommend that you find a yoga teacher capable of teaching these methods to you rather than attempting them alone. This is because, performed incorrectly or without adequate preparation, they may be harmful.

The easiest form of Pranayama for a beginner is Ujjayi breathing. If you are not a practicing yogi, then it is best to restrict yourself to the following method, which I shall call "ujjayi-lite" for brevity. In essence, this is a simple method of deep breathing, which you may practice at any time.

First, ensure you are seated in a comfortable position, with your back reasonably erect, your chin tucked in, and the muscles of your lower belly engaged. Hold yourself in this position throughout your breathing practice.

Second, breathe out fully and deeply.

Third, allow your breath to enter through your nostrils, entirely filling your lungs. Imagine this happening first as filling your belly, then imagine it as filling both sides and the back of your chest, then lastly as filling your entire chest up to your collar bones. Do not hold your breath.

Fourth, breathe out deeply and fully through your nostrils.

Repeat the Third and Fourth stages for as long as you are able to concentrate on doing so. While you are breathing in this way, continually check that your position is as it should be, and that your shoulders are relaxed. If you feel light-headed or in any way uncomfortable then cease immediately and return to normal breathing. Do not practice breath retention in any form unless a qualified yogi is present.

MEDITATION

Benefits of Meditation

The following are all generally accepted benefits of meditation:

Develops intuition

Releases subconscious fears and blockages

Promotes clarity of mind, thought, and speech

Improves ability to stay focussed, enhancing efficiency

Breaks stress-producing habit patterns

Promotes a sense of well-being and inner peace

Produces mental stability

Encourages self-confidence, self-reliance, self-mastery

Expands perception from daily to the infinite (divine)

The ability to meditate is also an absolute pre-requisite for communicating with your higher self and therefore for any form of healing.

If you lack experience in meditation, simply follow the guidelines below. Ensure you set yourself a clear intention: this avoids having a wishy-washy, unfocused experience. Once set and verbalized, you may forget it and focus on the rest of the methodology below.

Do not follow my process slavishly: use your intuition freely and vary the process as you feel best fits you.

Meditation Practice

PREPARATION

Sit comfortably
Ensure you are balanced, your back is upright but
allowed to retain its natural curves
Relax your shoulders, broaden your collarbones
Keep your chin tucked in and the back of your neck
slightly extended
You are upright but relaxed

Set yourself an intention. [This could be simply to relax, or it could be you want an answer to a question perplexing you. Form the intention clearly in words and speak it internally]

Set yourself a timescale for the meditation

Relax your face and especially your eyes

Relax your whole body, imagining a wave of relaxation spreading downwards

Close your eyes and allow your body to fall still

BREATHING

Breathe steadily, noticing where you feel your breath (nostril, back of throat, chest, etc)

Do not force your breath in any way

Bring your attention to the bridge between your nostrils

Observe the ebb and flow of your breath

Let the breath become smooth and calm

BECOMING PRESENT

Bring your attention to your breath

(Calm breathing, not forced)

Slightly deepen your breath

Picture your breath circling, or in waves

Focus on the sound of your breath as it enters and
departs your nostrils

Now focus on the feel and/or the sound of your breath
within your nostrils

Now focus on the momentary pause in movement as
your breath transitions from in to out, and from out to in

BASIC MEDITATION

You are now fully conscious of your breath

Keeping your mind clear, let any sounds wash over you,
through you, or around you.

Thoughts or feelings will arise. Do not be concerned. As
soon as you recognise their presence, simply let them
move freely through your mind

As thoughts depart, observe it with calmness and return
your attention to your breath

ENDING

Your intuition will tell you when your intended timescale is reached

It is best to take a few moments to breathe quietly and deeply before opening your eyes. And then to remain calm and move slowly and with deliberation for a few more minutes

SPIRITUALITY

Scientific Enigmas

Our eyes and other senses tell us that the world is made up of solid matter. Science supposedly tells us that truth and therefore knowledge is only gained when theories have been confirmed through rigorous testing. Unfortunately, it is only logically possible to use testing to deny a theory not to confirm it, since some other as yet unknown test may be discovered.

Newtonian physics tells us our world is made up of laws such as cause and effect, gravity, space and time, and so on. Unfortunately, quantum mechanics also tells us that at least at a sub-atomic level an object is affected by the act of perceiving by a subject.

Universal Energy

Fortunately there is a way to understand all the above. We believe our minds result somewhat mysteriously from the activity of our brains. This concept is broadly known as dualism. Whereas, the opposite is true. The physical world is created by our minds or, more correctly, by our collective Mind energy.

We are all a part of this universal energy, one and indivisible with it, both originally and in our present physical form. Thus we all interact and communicate directly with it, since we are part of it. For some reason this truth is commonly referred to as non-dualism.

Certain 'laws' are required in order to make sense of the physical world, but they are illusory. With sufficient practice, we are able to regain our ability to bypass these illusions and gain direct experience of the world as it truly exists. Pure, universal, vibrational energy, of which we are all a part.

As we gain in sensitivity, so we realise that our words and thoughts become reality. This means that as we develop our sensibility, we must be careful what we allow ourselves to think or ponder upon.

Brain Waves

The frequency of our brain waves varies according to the nature of activity our brains are performing. Below are the generally accepted classifications of brain waves:

Frequency	Name	Activity
28 to 5,000 Hz	Gamma	Higher (concentrating)
14 to 28 Hz	Beta	Active, alert thinking and talking

7 to 14 Hz	Alpha	Relaxed, meditative state
4 to 7 Hz	Theta	Very deep relaxation, meditation
0 to 4 Hz	Beta	Sleep

A gong bath should lead your brain into an Alpha state quite readily. It may also lead you into a Theta state, at which point you typically experience patterns or colours. In many instances it will also lead you into a Beta state.

Psychic Senses

Your chakras and psychic senses may also be enlivened or enriched during a gong bath. In particular, you may experience activity in the areas listed below.

This activity is often felt for the first time as a slight swirling or queasiness, or even indigestion. The corresponding effect is noted. For example, if you feel any activity around your third eye (approx. centre of your forehead), then you may have some kind of clairvoyant experience or realise that you have clairvoyant capabilities.

Solar Plexus	Empathy
Third Eye	Clairvoyance
Above Ears	Clairaudience
Crown	Revelation, prediction

ABOUT THE AUTHOR

Stephen Hill teaches yoga, sound and energy healing, mainly in the UK. He performs healing only upon select individual clients or during retreats, and holds qualifications in Reiki and other forms of healing.

Stephen holds an Honours degree in Philosophy from the University of Kent at Canterbury, and advises on the ethics and application of Artificial Intelligence in business and government.

He is a qualified RYA Yachtmaster and an active kayaker. He is also a Fellow of the RSA (FRSA) and a father of three adult children. He has published a number of books under a pseudonym.

More information on Stephen is available at www.yogisurivandana.com

Printed in Great Britain
by Amazon